Baby Boy Phoenix

Baby Boy Phoenix

A Tale of Rescue,
Love,
and Second Chances

by Jenny Karns

With Contributions from Toby Wisneski,
Mary Ann Hart, Chester, and Baby Boy Phoenix

Dreality Press

Baby Boy Phoenix: A Tale of Rescue, Love, and Second Chances.

by Jenny Karns

Published by Dreality Press

11333 N. Moorpark Blvd #35 Studio City, CA 91602

First Edition, 2014

Published in the United States of America

DEDICATION

Phoenix and I want to dedicate this book to every human who has ever loved a dog and every dog who has ever loved a human. You are the people and the animals changing the world for the good, tipping the scales, and making a difference.

We love you and appreciate you!
Dog/God bless

And to Buster and Chester and Phoenix:
You kicked the door of my heart open and never let it shut.
I am entirely changed and eternally grateful.

Mommy loves you forever!!

ACKNOWLEDGMENTS

There are so many people to acknowledge and give thanks to when it comes to Baby Boy Phoenix and the creation of this book about his journey.

I want to first thank our dear readers and editors: Heather DeSisto, Liza Botkin, Ilana Orea, Dave Karns, and Lynn Karns. Thank you to our photographer, Frank Wisneski, for the awesome cover photo as well as a few of the most beautiful interior shots.

We are so very grateful for the loving wishes and support of the Baby Boy Phoenix Facebook community. Without your asking for the book in the first place, checking in, sending love and prayers, and being, in general, the very best community of support, this book would have never even been imagined!
You are the wind beneath our wings and the awesome co~manifestors of this project!

A huge debt of gratitude goes to Leave No Paws Behind. In particular CEO and founder Toby Wisneski, without whom, Phoenix would not have survived. He would have been a bright star in the heavens but, due to Toby's efforts, he is a bright star in all of our lives. Endless appreciation goes to East Valley Veterinary Clinic, doctors Mary Ann Hart and Mark Hohne, and the amazing team of vets and technicians that started the Phoenix love and healing fest! Endless thanks to every person who donated to Baby Boy Phoenix's care and recovery. Your energy, in the form of money, prayers, and selfless love changed the course of this baby boy's life forever.

To everyone who works in rescue and recovery, we give thanks. You are angels who are sorely needed.

Love,
Jenny Karns and Baby Boy Phoenix

Baby Boy Phoenix

Chapter 1
IN THE BEGINNING

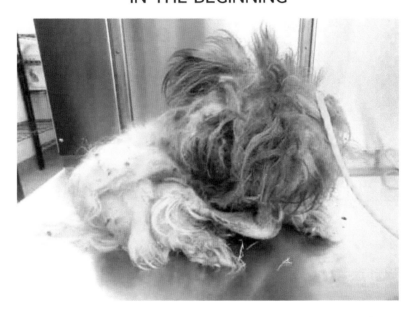

"Being indigenous the Phoenix represents rebirth, from the ashes from a past life of turmoil. To be reborn in spirit from brokenness and be made whole of heart, to look and walk forward with no ill will, but to rize up and be beautiful once again from the heart....To Rize up from the ashes is to live once again, as your Phoenix has with your love.....xo"

~LeeAnna LongWolf

Jenny Karns:

Baby Boy Phoenix's forever Mom

I do not know where Phoenix came from or what happened to him before his arrival at the Orange County Animal Shelter on June 5th, 2013. Since he was surrendered to the shelter as a "stray" with no other information, we are left with only suppositions as to the causes of his extreme neglect, starvation, and injuries.

What I do know of the facts of his story are these: He was rescued the following day from the shelter by Leave No Paws Behind, a charitable organization dedicated to finding care for senior and special needs animal rescues. LNPB found the exemplary medical care Phoenix needed at East Valley Veterinary Clinic where he was treated for his malnutrition and infections. It was when he first arrived at East Valley that Toby, the founder of LNPB, named him Baby Boy Phoenix and prayed he would live up to his name. Phoenix did live up to his name! After two weeks at East Valley, he went to the foster home of woman named Carol Sax. For two weeks he lived there, growing healthier and stronger. On July 1^{st,} he came to his forever home where he now lives with me and his Lhasa Apso brother, Chester. I officially adopted Phoenix on July 6th.

When he first arrived at the vets office on June 6th, he was very weak. He was skin and bones under the mounds of matted hair that covered his eyes and kept one of his hurt legs bound to his chest. The mats were full of maggots and the maggots had caused sores on his body. The maggots had also gotten inside a wound on his foot and were eating away at the bones.

I talked to one vet tech who said he shuddered when he saw the X-Rays of Phoenix's foot. "There were bones literally missing where there should have been bones. They were eaten away" he told me.

The vets planned to amputate the leg as soon as Phoenix grew strong enough. A surgery would have been too hard on him when they first rescued him so they needed to wait until he grew stronger. They wrapped the paw and did everything else they could for him to recover.

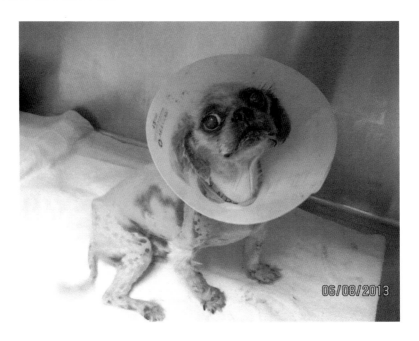

06/08/2013

What I do know, beyond the facts of this story, is that a whole new life began for Phoenix and for me the day

LNPB pulled him from the shelter. He was given the opportunity to rise out of the ashes of his previous life and to be born again, healthier and stronger, and even more lovable after the rise. Phoenix was made new that day. His picture went out on Facebook where over 40 thousand viewers saw him and loved him. Where he had possibly never received love, he was now receiving and bathing in the healing love of thousands, and most especially the direct love of Toby. She reminded him that his life was worth it and that he was loved. His old life was washed away and the possibility of a new one ready to begin.

Since then he has overcome mountains of trauma both physically and emotionally. His paw has healed entirely and he walks on it now without issue. Best of all, he is now calm and stress free. He eats well. He plays hard, and he loves everyone. No exception. Every person who comes to the door, or that we meet on the street, is greeted with as big a hug as they will allow from this little angel. In fact, he loves people so much, and is such a good healer boy, that I am now certifying him to be a therapy dog so he can share his gift of love with people who are hospitalized, homebound, or convalescing and really need Phoenix's contagious energy and love for their own healing.

He has truly risen from the ashes and is the happiest boy as well as an inspiration to all who greet him. I know he feels exceptionally lucky and blessed and so do I. He changed my life and expanded my heart. He is a constant teacher about what it means to survive and thrive and to love unconditionally despite hardships, disappointments, and sufferings. Phoenix has taught me that love always wins over evil and the magic of true freedom lies in being present and loving every moment.

Those who know me and know Phoenix's story believe I did something to rescue Phoenix, where in fact his amazing heart and spirit has just as equally rescued me. Rescue dog rescued me. I am eternally grateful to be the primary recipient of the blessed love of Phoenix, the beloved baby joy boy with a heart of gold.

Chapter 2
THE HEART OF A VET

"Bless his sweet and forgiving little heart....it is so good to see how he's come round....Thanks to East Valley Veterinary and the ANGELS at Leave No Paws Behind."

~Dorothy Freeman

"God Bless You Dr. Hart!"

~Deborah C Moes Cass

Mary Ann Hart D.V.M.

Phoenix's first vet at East Valley Veterinary Clinic

After working with Toby and Leave No Paws Behind for two years, I was becoming quite experienced in dealing with LNPB's 'scruffy' collection of dogs presented to me at East Valley Veterinary Clinic for evaluation and treatment. However, when I first saw Baby Boy Phoenix even I held an inward gasp. He was in deplorable condition, emaciated, filthy, and with open wounds encompassing a front leg, which was twisted and useless. Once I moved beyond the visceral reaction at his appearance and proceeded through my exam, I felt a little excitement. There was hope underneath it all.

The shelter had been concerned that his limb was infected with bone cancer based on X-rays, which would also account for his emaciation. This was a real possibility, but bone cancer in dogs is notoriously quick to spread to the lungs and our chest X-rays of Baby Boy were clear. Severe infection in the bone can look identical to bone cancer, but I had never seen anything that widespread and destructive to the bone from an infection.

He had other problems: a loud heart murmur, anemia, a high white blood cell count, and dangerously low blood proteins. His abnormalities were all explainable by severe infection and starvation. We continued treatments that the shelter had begun such as antibiotics and pain medications, and we threw in more: Vitamin B-12 injections, oral iron supplement, and additional pain control and antibiotics. His leg required bandage protection and support. One of the best things I remember that happened the first day I saw him was that he *ate food* for us! That willingness was a huge victory, and at that point we knew we just had to be patient.

As he kept eating and his energy increased I knew his chances for recovery were getting a tiny bit better day by day. His spirit and personality were stellar, and everyone at East Valley began to feel the satisfaction of knowing he *would* recover and have the life of a well-loved pet, which he sorely deserved and would receive, thanks to LNPB. After two weeks his blood work normalized and his heart murmur disappeared. He was gaining weight and was a wonderful patient, despite all the administrations he required. He never complained and he was happy and friendly, despite what humans had dealt him in the past.

Eventually he was strong enough to leave East Valley and go to a foster home. He was still terribly thin and his leg useless, but the sores were healing. Our original plan was to amputate his diseased limb once he was physically able to withstand the surgery. I was not hopeful that the leg would ever be useful given the damage to the bones seen on X-ray, and that it would be non-functional and a source of pain for the rest of his life. Of course, Baby Boy had other ideas, and his limb healed and eventually he could use it. That remains the biggest medical mystery of Baby Boy's story that still surprises me. I am grateful he proved me wrong about his leg and it's very satisfying to know he has the love and protection of a family now.

Chapter 3
THE WILL TO SURVIVE

"A true miracle--who would have believed that poor pup would survive? Not many people would believe that anyone would put the time, money, and energy into trying to get him to recover? LNPB believed. That's who! They rallied around him and placed their healing hands on him. Slowly he started to rise higher and higher. Thousands prayed for him. The power of the pack touched him, loved him and healed him. Today he knows love and lots of it! He is one of many that LNPB has touched with their miracle hands. One of many that the village held in their loving arms. He is what LNPB is all about. Loved by tens of thousands who will never forget that little fur ball that touched our hearts. Having Jenny and Chester is the cherry on the top!"

~Kathy Kobilis

Toby Wisneski:

CEO/Founder of Leave No Paws Behind

You cannot say "miracle", "will to live", "believe" or "amazing medical transformation" without three little words coming to mind, "Baby Boy Phoenix."

I will never, ever forget how my heart just cracked when I first met this most darling and loving lil man who had such a strong will to live and the spirit of an angel. He came to us with no name and it did not take us long before we knew he was a "Phoenix," who we prayed one day would rise above the ashes. He was severely emaciated and had a deformed leg that was riddled with bone infection and disease.

The tears just flowed at the thought of what this precious lil man had endured in his short little life. I remember the good Doc telling me "We are taking it one day at a time." I also remember the sleepless and worrisome nights we all had, praying that this lil guy would somehow rally.

Well then it happened. Our prayers were answered and with the wonderful medical care he was receiving, BBP turned the corner. He was by no means out of the woods but the Doc was now "cautiously optimistic" that this lil fella was on his way to a complete recovery. We were not sure that he would be able to keep his leg. He was still too emaciated and his blood work was questionable, so he could not undergo surgery at that time.

BBP was now ready for his second leg to recovery. I reached out to one of our amazing and loving human angel fosters, Carole, to ask if she could help. Without hesitation, she stepped right up! Phoenix went on to spend the next several weeks in her care, thriving and getting better with each passing day! The medicine he was on began working and before long he was up and playing and using that leg!

He was now ready for his third and what would be his final leg to recovery, a long term foster. I was contacted by another amazing and loving human angel, Jenny Karns and as we all know, the rest is history!

With an enormous amount of prayers, love, medical care, and his strong spirit and will to live, BBP went on, not only to heal, but to find his forever home! His leg was no longer riddled with infection or disease, his blood work was perfect and he is now a "superstar" with his own FB page and one of the many, many reasons we continue to do what we do! LNPB is so proud of our #1 medically transformed rescue of 2013, Baby Boy Phoenix, who did indeed rise so very high above the ashes! Here at LNPB, the rescue never ends with the pull.

Chapter 4
RESTORED BELIEF

"Dogs do speak, but only to those who know how to listen."
~Orhan Pamuk, My Name is Red

Phoenix:

When Toby first held me in her arms I knew I was safe. I had never known so much love! She told me that I mattered. I thought she said "matted" because... I was...

But then she said it again... "Mattered."

This was a bigger word than anyone ever said to me before and it made me feel very big inside and strong!

I mattered.

She also told me I would be ok and that made me feel less afraid. I was worried there for a while. It grew very dark and hard to see when the mats covered my eyes. I was starving and sick and I thought I would surely die but Toby showed me the light. She cut me free from death's hold and she named me Phoenix! How could she ever know that that was my true name?! It was a miracle!

I was told once that in order to survive in this life I would have to believe in love and miracles. I do now!

Toby was my miracle #1.

I believe.

Chapter 5
OVERCOMING LOSS AND LOVING ONCE AGAIN

"It came to me that every time I lose a dog, they take a piece of my heart with them. And every new dog who comes into my life gifts me with a piece of their heart. If I live long enough, all the components of my heart will be dog, and I will become as generous and loving as they are."

~Unknown

Jenny:

I had been following Leave No Paws Behind on Facebook for a few years before Phoenix came to me. I am always so inspired by all of the stories shared there of rescued animals that are medical emergencies or elderly. Toby pulls the dogs, sight unseen, and gets them the medical care they need to have a second chance. In the cases where they cannot overcome the traumas or sicknesses, she holds them and tells them that their life has been worth it as they pass over the rainbow bridge into that special light made just for the beautiful creatures like these. It's such a gift she gives to these precious angels who continue to love, no matter what form of shameful thing any human has ever done to them.

I know Toby's work is incredibly hard but also so rewarding. Even in the hardest moments when you have to let a dog go over the rainbow bridge, it is an absolute honor to hold them as they pass. In that moment they pass to us a blessing of pure love.

When I first started following Toby, I was grieving the loss of my 12 year old Shepherd, Buster. I had the honor of holding him and looking into his eyes as he passed into the light. I was still seeing Buster everywhere and feeling him next to me when I slept, but then I would wake up and he wasn't there.

Luckily I still had my other puppy love, a 13 year old Lhasa Apso named Chester. Chester made it very clear to me after Buster died that he was happy to have his mommy all to himself. "No other doggies Mom!" was the words I heard him speaking to me in my head.

"Are you sure Chester? So many need homes." But then he would roll over and look away from me as if to say... "I'm old now. I put in my time. I don't want to have to deal with another dog."

I respected his wishes because I loved him so much, but I threw the half of my expanded heart that Buster had left wide open with his amazing life and love, into following the dogs on Leave No Paws Behind. Every week I would pray and wish and send good thoughts and money for their healing! And the best part was that I got to do this with a community of other animal lovers! Together we were stronger and the magic that occurred in the lives of so many dogs over that year, through that community, and because of Toby was palpable! It was also a powerful lesson for me in what we can create when we come together as a community and what kind of healing is possible with a good dose of unconditional love. It's that love that the dogs give us so freely and here was an opportunity to give it back to them. What an honor!

Then one day, Toby posted a picture of the dog soon to be named Phoenix. He was just a mass of matted hair. The picture popped up on my computer with a message that she was taking him to the vet to see if he could be saved. Even though he was a mess and entirely unrecognizable as being a dog, I thought… "That's my boy!"

I also had the second thought that of course it couldn't be because Chester would never allow it. Plus this sick doggie might not even survive the trip to the vet. He did, however, make it to the vet where they shaved him down to the skin to treat the maggot wounds and wrapped his wounded leg. They were trying to get him strong before they amputated the leg but they were "cautiously optimistic" at the vet that he would even survive. But he did survive and every day I watched, along with the rest of the community, his amazing progress and waited with bated breath for every new picture and update.

And more than merely surviving, he seemed happy! Even when he was clearly in pain he seemed to smile for the camera as if to say "Look at my lucky life now! Whoohooo!". He loved everyone and charmed his way into the hearts of Toby, all the vets, and of course the online community because he was so happy and loving and forgiving despite all he had been through. He was given the name Baby Boy Phoenix, the dog who was rising from the ashes.

A few weeks into Phoenix's recovery, Toby posted that he would be up for adoption soon. Before I could stop myself I was writing her a letter! We talked and she agreed that I could foster him for a few days so we could see how Chester did with him and if Phoenix would take to me and Chester. I do healing work and I knew that even if I only had a few days with him before Chester said no, I could at LEAST help his leg and hopefully maybe he could keep that paw!

Later that day, I picked a tarot card as my way of asking the universe, God, the great energy of life, whatever you want to call it, what I needed to know spiritually about Phoenix coming to stay with me. I got the card for school and education. I understood immediately that I would be learning some very important and powerful things from this angel boy. Later that day, I passed a sign for the "University of Phoenix" and I giggled! Phoenix was coming and I would be entering the metaphorical University of Baby Boy Phoenix! What fun!!

The next day I was so nervous and excited as I got everything ready for Phoenix to come over! I talked to Chester about it and explained Phoenix's situation and I also told him, he was my number one man. It was ultimately up to him to tell me if Phoenix could stay.

Needless to say, it worked out and the boys loved each other. They often sleep in the same bed together and cuddle. Chester acts like a whole new dog even at the age of 15 now! Phoenix has brought so much love and joy into both of our lives and Buster led the way. We can all feel it. He is our angel on the other side.

I am constantly inspired by the eternal and pure love of dogs. The fact that DOG is GOD spelled backwards does not escape me. I am a humble and joyful student of that love. I love the quote and meditate on it often: "It came to me that every time I lose a dog, they take a piece of my heart with them. And every new dog who comes into my life gifts me with a piece of their heart. If I live long enough, all the components of my heart will be dog, and I will become as generous and loving as they are."

No one seems to know who said this quote but any of us who have known the love of a dog could easily add our names to it! I tell the boys all the time, "You are my whole heart!" And it's true. Anything that is good and pure and loving was planted there by God and then nurtured by my dogs.

Chapter 6
A STAR IS BORN!

"This boy and his story bring me so much joy. I love his Facebook page!"

~Gina Stephens

Jenny:

When Phoenix came to live with me, many of the people who had so lovingly followed him on Toby's Leave No Paws Behind Facebook page, asked that I make Phoenix his own page so that they could follow his progress. I resisted initially thinking, "A Facebook page for a dog?" However I then realized that for all the time and energy I had spent following him, I would be devastated if he were adopted by someone else and I was not able to continue to see his progress!

He was no longer "just a dog" and of course I never believed he was, but what I found out was that he was also a movement. Good people needed good news and Phoenix was that. He was a miracle play by play and people wanted to tune in! Plus, anyone who is an animal lover or animal rights activist sees so much bad news every day. It's comforting and means our activists lives mean something and make a difference when we see dogs like Baby Boy Phoenix, growing beyond the trauma and experiencing a life full of happiness.

After making the Facebook page for him, it was revolutionary for me to see the amount of love and support that showed up for this one little dog as well as for me and Chester too. Then Phoenix began to write posts and I began to write some as well. It was through the encouragement and support of that community that this book was called forth!

Here is one of the first posts on Baby Boy Phoenix's Facebook page from July 5, 2013:

Lessons from Phoenix:

1. Forgive and love... repeatedly and consistently!

2. Get out and hug your neighbors! You never know who's just around the corner that's ready to love you like crazy.

3. Play hard, sleep deep, eat well, and pay attention. There are so many good things happening. Don't miss the sweet stuff. :))

A grateful word from Jenny:

Phoenix is such a sweet little teacher! He RUNS to hug all the neighbors and everyone he meets has been so inspired by him and his story. He got us invited to a BBQ yesterday by fixating on two women walking across the street and not breaking eye contact with them! It was like he was saying, "Where are you going without hugging me?"

They eventually got pulled across the street to meet us and he melted into their arms while we all chatted. Phoenix is making us some new and LOVELY friends. He always has an eye on me but it's like he knows that the whole world loves him now and all is well.

His foot is doing great! He uses it and then picks it up if it's bothering him. He's sleeping through the night curled up next to Chester and he has a million nap spots around the house from chairs to beds to couches. He is taking full advantage of what it feels like to have a HOME. It makes me so happy to see him this content. Even when sleeping, if I move at all, he looks up and blinks at me. He's always paying attention, always ready to run over for a hug, kiss, or snuggle. Always ready to be loved.

Lesson #4: Always be ready to be loved.

Thank you, community, for your outpouring of love for this guy. He feels it. I feel it. You all are healing him. Please keep up your prayers that the infection clears in his leg so he can keep it!! Much love to you each and have a super blessed and happy day! Don't forget to hug a neighbor. Xoxoxo

Chapter 7
HEARTS AND STARS

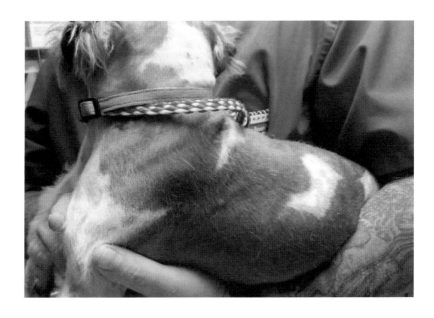

"If you pick up a starving dog and make him prosperous, he will not bite you. This is the principal difference between a dog and a man."

~Mark Twain

Jenny:

The first few days after Phoenix came to live with me he was still mostly skin with a few little hairs starting to poke through. The docs had shaved him down to the skin to get all the mats off. Then they had to treat the skin wounds from where the maggots had invaded and infected him. He had a little fuzz on top of his head, but otherwise he was all skin and scabs. It was the middle of the summer and it was hot in Los Angeles all the time. Plus he was still burning the infections out of his body so his little body was constantly on fire! He wanted to be close to me all the time and cuddled up so I ran the air a lot that month trying to keep both of us cool enough to get some real healing happening!

He slept a lot at first, but not deeply. He was anxious, still traumatized, and worried about everything. He was happiest and most content when close to my body. Like a newborn baby I kept him constantly close even joking that I might need to get one of those mommy wraps that straps the babies to the mom's body! Luckily I work from home doing massage and healing work, as well as writing, so I had the ability to spend a lot of time with him. When I did the healing work, he would sleep at my feet soaking up the good vibes. When I wrote, he lay across my lap snoring away. When I was in motion, he curled up with Chester and they nursed each other.

Just a few weeks before Phoenix's arrival, Chester had had eleven teeth removed. The operation and medications had weakened his immune system and he developed an auto immune reaction where his paws and the skin on his back and around his eyes became raw and bled. His vet had put him on some steroids to stop the skin issues and wrapped all four of his feet to let them heal. He was on the mend when Phoenix came to us, but was still recovering, as was Phoenix.

Somehow through their shared need to heal and mend, they bonded. Phoenix took to Chester right away and Chester, to my surprise, let him! Phoenix would press his whole body into a bed right up close to Chester. Chester, who had always been very independent, sighed his approval. It seemed Phoenix was accepted and even more than accepted, dare I say... loved!

It was in the comfort of his brother's arms, and bed, that I found Phoenix on day three, with lots of tiny hairs starting to poke through his little naked skin and the most amazing pattern beginning to emerge on his back.

By the next day I could make out a heart and a diamond and what looked like a star! His skin had been grey when first shaved, but now it was patchy and growing in brown with a white heart, a star, and a diamond!

Our BBP was coming into his own and his skin and new fur were growing in like a storybook illustration of his transformation story. Here he was, a diamond in the rough, with a beautiful big heart, from the stars and clearly meant to be a star!

Chapter 8
FINDING HOME

"Baby boy, you are safe! You will forever be happy and loved, tickled and scratched, and have food and treats...life is so wonderful. Go run and play!"

~Rowann Gilman

Phoenix:

I was so scared leaving Toby and all the vets at East Valley. I had been so sick and they had taken such good care of me. They gave me a bed of my very own and treats and lots of love. I loved everyone there, especially Toby.

Toby told me everything would be OK. She told me that I would be going to a loving foster mommy's house to get better and then they would find me a real forever home. A real forever home? I couldn't even imagine it, but it sounded glorious when she talked and I wasn't scared anymore.

I rested and started getting stronger while I was at foster Mommy Carol's house. She was so kind to me. I liked living in a home.

Then came the day to go see Jenny and Chester! I heard about them but I didn't know what to expect. Would they be the forever home that Toby talked about? I hoped so! I never had a real mommy or brother before.

When I arrived, Jenny opened the car door to greet me. She took me in her arms and I felt home. I could feel her heart beating and I knew she was mine.

Toby was Miracle #1 and now new Mommy Jenny was Miracle #2.

Then when we went inside, I thought I was in heaven! There were dog beds and toys everywhere!! I ran around to all of them using my good three legs. I rolled around on my back in utter joy and then I threw the toys around too!

At one point I ran into the kitchen and that's when I found him.... Chester! He was in the kitchen by the food bowl and we greeted each other. He didn't seem so sure about me at first, but I loved him right away. He looked kinda like me if I had hair and I was sure we could be friends... even brothers!

When I got tired, the new Jenny mommy held me and cuddled me. It felt so safe in her arms. I could feel warmth coming out of her hands as she placed them on my hurt paw and I knew she was healing me.

All the excitement made me tired. For a few days, all I wanted to do was sleep. So from bed to bed, mom to Chester, couch to chair, and back to a bed again... I rested and recovered. I could relax here.

I was home.

Chapter 9
A BROTHER'S LOVE

"Love is a book written only by those brave enough to turn the page."

~Michael Xaxier

Chester:

Phoenix's fifteen year old Lhasa Apso Brother

I was a little nervous, but actually secretly glad when my mom started telling me about Phoenix. She had been so sad since Buster died and even though the two of us got more quality time together, I have to admit that I was slowing down and wouldn't be able to keep an eye on my mom forever. Especially with this eye sight loss... Much harder to keep an eye on her now!

I do always keep an ear on her though. My favorite thing is to be near my mom when she is with clients. I like listening to her voice and when she says something very important, I snore really loudly. It's my way of saying "Amen, Mom! Yes!" I snore out agreements like a good gospel congregation. She can tend to be quiet, my mom, and I want her to use her voice more so when she does, I chime in my support in the form of an excessively loud snore. She seems to understand because she giggles at this and explains to her clients that I am a vibrational healer and the snores are all part of the therapy. She's right. It's true, but mostly I snore to support her. She's my #1 priority. I was born to be her dog and when my body gives out and can no longer snore, support, and cuddle her, I will be her angel.

My brother Buster is our angel. He left his body over a year before Phoenix came to live with us. I pushed my face in his neck, the night it happened, and then nudged his nose which made his head flop to the side. He was gone. But then I felt him fill up the whole room with his love and I thought to him, "Oh Buster, how did you get so BIG?" And he thought back to me, "I've always been big, little dog, but now I'm free."

I was sad without his big warm body and his unwavering eyesight, but I still felt him close to me and mom did too. He said he worried about me, but I told him not to. I was fine and I would take good care of the Mom now.

But after a year I worried how long I could keep it up. The surgery to have my teeth out was exhausting and then my paws got all bloody and sore. All that scared me. Who would take care of mom if something happened to me?

One day she asked me about Phoenix and I said yes! She
didn't seem to believe me at first but I said, "yes, yes, yes!"
over and over again until she listened. I hoped that he was
the one Buster had been telling me about. The one that was
to come who I could train on all the best ways to watch over
and love the mom.

But would I have enough time???

When Phoenix arrived I felt instantly at ease. He was a sweet
dog. Other dogs can be impatient with me as I am an old man
now. I run into things and frustrate them. But Phoenix didn't
seem to mind and he cuddled up close to me. I could sense
that he was healing from something too. We were instant
brothers in our need to heal and joint love for the mom. He
loved her right away too and that was all that mattered to me.

I was relieved. Buster had sent us the perfect dog. I would
have help looking after the mom now. This was good because

I was having a hard time breathing and waking up in the middle of the night to pace around. Mom woke up and sat with me trying to calm me down. One night it was just too much. I couldn't get a breath and I started coughing up blood. Mom rushed me to the hospital where they took me away from her, gave me meds, and put me in an oxygen tank.

I was too weak to notice anything for a few days... except the angels. There were so many angels all watching over me. Buster was there of course and all these people I had never seen before, all praying for me to get better. One angel asked if I was ready to go home.

"Home to Mom?" I asked?

"No home to the light" she said, "home to Buster and the realms of the angels."

"Oh, no thank you." I said. "I'm not ready for that yet. See... I have a new brother and I have to teach him everything I know before I go to the light. I also worry that if I left now my mom would think it was her fault for getting Phoenix and stressing me out. He doesn't stress me out, but she doesn't know that yet. I have to go home and show her I approve and love him. I haven't had enough time with them as a family yet. Please. Just a little more time, angels...."

On the third day my mom was there with her arm in the oxygen tank when I woke up. I suddenly felt better in my body. The doc came in and I barked at the doc to let me go home. I barked and barked. I haven't had a need to bark in years, so I surprised my mom I think, but I really wanted them to understand that I needed to go home. The doc said it was OK and Mom carried me out of there. It felt so good to be in her arms again.

When I got home, Phoenix was so happy to see me that he peed all over himself. Kids! It made my heart swell though, nonetheless. I had more time with them. I would use it well and live every day to the fullest. I would teach Phoenix everything I knew. I would get to love my mommy for more days.

More days to love. That's what life is all about. More days to live and love.

Chapter 10
THE DARK NIGHT

"Prayers from Michigan to you and your sweet babies! Thank you for your heart....I am beyond happy BB Phoenix is with you!"

~Lindsay Hubbard Fall

"Until one has loved an animal, a part of one's soul remains unawakened."

~Anatole France

Jenny:

I was terrified the night Chester coughed up blood. We rushed out to the emergency vet and I prayed the whole way, as I also tried to soothe and calm him so he would not hyperventilate out of fear.

It was not our normal vet and this doctor was gruff. He referred to Chester as "That dog" rather than as Chester or even, "your dog," but "that doctor" kept my boy alive and I am grateful.

It didn't look good that night as there was a lot of fluid in Chester's lungs and his heart was enlarged. When I got home I sobbed into Phoenix's neck and posted on Phoenix's Facebook that we could use some prayers. I tossed and turned all night, unable to sleep. When sleep finally came in the wee morning hours I dreamt about angels surrounding me, so many people I had never known, praying for me and my boys. In the morning when I woke up, I found over three hundred messages on Baby Boy Phoenix's Facebook page offering love, prayers, and support. The angels were real people and I was overcome for the second time within twelve hours.

I phoned the doc as soon as they were officially open to get a report on Chester. The diagnosis was pneumonia which was treatable if he could withstand treatment at his age. The meds he had been on for his teeth surgery and then subsequent auto immune reaction had weakened his immune system and that was how he got the pneumonia in the first place. Now he would have to take a hand-full of new meds every day to clear the pneumonia. As a holistic practitioner, this was far harder for me to swallow than Chester and if he survived this, he would have to swallow those pills for six to eight subsequent weeks.

He would also have to be on oxygen for at least a few more days which meant he had to stay at the hospital. I hated leaving him there, but meanwhile there was a Phoenix doggie at home that was comforting me and who was also very worried himself. I saw how obviously confused and upset he was in Chester's absence and I understood very deeply that this pup was not a temporary visitor. He was family and this was his home.

I phoned Toby and let her know that I would no longer just be fostering Phoenix. I wanted to be his forever home if she would allow it.

Chapter 11
ADOPTION DAY
July 6th, 2013

"CONGRATULATIONS! Happiest news ever!!!
Little Phoenix, you make my heart smile and I am more happy for
you than you will ever know! You deserve all the love and care and
very best of everything in the whole wide world. You have such a
beautiful and amazing spirit ... you are an incredible survivor ...
and you make us all so happy that you have come into our hearts.
Love you so much! Happy furever life, Little Dude!"
~Sharon Hines

Phoenix's words on Facebook:

Mommy just talked to Toby and it's official!! I have a forever home!! Thank you all for your love and prayers and helping me find so much love and happiness!! I'm feeling great and using my leg. It looks like I will get to keep it as long as that infection clears up which it seems to be doing. The vet will tell Mommy more in a month, but for now, thank you for your healing prayers. You are the best support a little dude like me could have ever hoped for!!

Toby's words on Facebook:

Just thirty short days ago I held and welcomed into my heart, this little, tiny, emaciated and abused little man. I kissed his little nose and promised him that nothing or no one was ever going to harm him again. He did not have a name, so I called him "Phoenix" and whispered to him over and over again, "we are all here to help you rise above the ashes." I let him know that here at LNPB we were always only a heartbeat away and that he had an entire Village of the most amazing and loving people praying and cheering him on. I can honestly say Phoenix gave me, as I am sure many of you as well, many a sleepless night fraught with worry. I can also attest to the fact that through it all, he always remained so happy and grateful to be alive! He had a fighting spirit and a strong will and desire to live! Today, thirty days later, our little man has truly risen high above the ashes and I am THRILLED to announce he now has a place to call home FOREVER with the most amazing and loving mommy who is also a long time Villager! I want to thank this entire Village from the bottom of my heart, for all your prayers, support, donations, and love because this little man would not be where he is today without all of you! Congratulations Baby Boy Phoenix, you are loved by so many and always remember that "Ms. Toby is always only a heartbeat away."

Chapter 12
CHESTER'S HAPPY HOMECOMING

"Glad the little family is back together again"!

~Mar Florida

"YAY! Super great news, I'm so happy for all of you, it makes me a bit weepy to read it all. Continued improved health to you and I'll continue to pray for you and send lots of love vibes. Just so very happy your little family is happily back together, yay for reunions! Xo"

~Lisa Burks

"What wonderful news!!! So glad everyone is home, happy, & healthy!"

~Sara Mynyk

Jenny:

After three days in the hospital, Chester was ready to come home to his mommy and brother and the reunion was beyond sweet!!

Facebook post by Jenny on July 8th, 2013:

Phoenix and I couldn't be happier!!!! Phoenix was so excited he slobbered all over him and then peed. **Oh sigh** I'll take it all and clean it all to have them both home and by my side!! Chester literally BUSTED out of there!! His late brother, Buster (a renowned escape artist), was smiling from above. The doc came to tell me they needed to keep him another night as he shoved his head out the hole allotted for my arm and started barking at her! Chester, who has not barked in 2 years (not had a good enough reason I guess) BARKED at the vet to let him go. She agreed that he was clearly off oxygen with his head out the hole and he was still doing great, no coughing or loss of color, and then we were free (After a hefty vet bill that is... yikes!). But even my sweet doc admitted that it was a MIRACLE how well he was doing!! I agree. And I can fully attest to the power of prayer and I am so grateful for EVERY ONE OF YOU ANGELS that has prayed my Phoenix and now my Chester into better health. Keep seeing and praying for the infection in Phoenix's leg to clear entirely and the infection in Chester's lungs cleared as well. It's a baby boy hospital over here but it is my honor to serve them. I have such deep respect for both of them and all of you. Sweet dreams when you get there and kiss all your pups for me! ~Jenny

Chapter 13
THE HEALING POWER OF LOVE

"A miraculous transformation. It's amazing to see what love can do!"

~Ellen Barbour Cole

Phoenix:

I was sleeping next to my brother one night when he started breathing funny. Then he started coughing. Mommy jumped up and within minutes they were out the door. I was so scared. The house was suddenly very quiet and I realized I had not yet been alone there in the week since I had arrived. There was always a warm body to snuggle up with and I suddenly felt very afraid. I looked around and found no one. They really had left!

Was Chester going to be ok? I already loved him so much and I didn't want him to go yet. I still had so much to learn from him!!

Later when Mommy came home, she was very upset, but she told me Chester was still alive and I was so relieved. I told her to tell our friends on Facebook because when they pray for puppies, puppies get better! I know! I was one of them!

When we went to bed, Mommy was still crying but I stayed close to her to reassure her that everything was going to be ok. Chester would be ok either way. If he didn't make it I would help her. I would love her enough for both of us. I began feeling much stronger while Chester was away because I was loving my mom so much and that love made me stronger.

When everybody prayed and sent love, I knew Chester would be ok the way I was, but now I was learning something new. I was healing myself and feeling better by loving too. I knew how much Chester loved Mommy. I hoped that he could heal by loving the same way I was.

Chester coming home was my miracle #3!

I would help him get strong by loving him! We would get strong together. I was already feeling so good that I began to believe that another miracle was possible. Maybe I would get to keep my leg!!

Chapter 14
LIFE GOES ON
AND WHAT A BEAUTIFUL LIFE IT IS

"What an inspiring little man with a huge heart! Thank you Phoenix for showing us all how to live." ~Dana Pallo

Beautiful words from an earth angel. Your inspiration touches every soul. You are very special and gifted and I recognize that as do we all. Thank you for sharing the soul you have been given with so many of us both animal and humans. You are a life teacher sent here to shown others the way. Bless you!! ~Marita Tilley

Phoenix's words on Facebook July 11th:

Good Morning everyone! I'm up on top of the desk in my mama's arms again today! I won't let her sit at the computer anymore without me. There is a window here and there is SO MUCH to see!! Birds and Squirrels and PEOPLE oh my!! My mom can't stop kissing me but I'm ok with that. My brother Chester is doing great today. He slept through the night with no coughing. I slept too!

We both ate a lot of food this morning. Mom shared her eggs. Yum!! OK, I gotta go. Squirrel!!!! I love you all!!! ~BBP

Jenny's words on Facebook on July 12th:

Hi All! It's Jenny reporting on behalf of Phoenix who is knocked out sound asleep beside me on one side, Chester on the other.

Phoenix had a big day playing with his friend Gilly at the pool and running around like a crazy happy puppy! His hair is growing in and his paw is doing great. If he runs a lot, he'll hobble later but he's good at sleeping a lot too and recovering. He just LOVES LIFE and wants to get every last juicy morsel out of everything he does! It's amazing. What a teacher he is! And he LOVES people! I had a chat with him today about maybe being a therapy dog. He has to be with me for three full months first so we'll talk about it more down the road... but I could tell he loved the idea. He is devoted to people and to healing and I know it would make him really happy to help people!! PLUS he's a HUGE inspiration, right?! I mean WE are all captivated by his heroic recovery and amazing ability to forgive and LOVE LOVE LOVE.

Chester is doing great. He seems to be recovering well from the pneumonia. Easy does it and steady progression. He's an older dude. He's been with me for 14 years now. We lost his 12 year old Shepherd/Lab mix brother a year and a half ago and we know that our angel Buster helped lead Phoenix to us. And Phoenix DOES things like Buster used to! It's wild!! He watches me and is in constant communication with me that he loves me and is ready for anything I'm ready for. He's earnest in his love. It's so dear.

I'm so grateful for all the angels (and I include each of you in that... and Toby and Buster and the Docs) who helped bring Phoenix into my life. I was sitting out front with Phoenix the other night when a man rode by on his bike. He stopped and looked at us and said, "Rescue Dog?" "Yes!" I replied. "I have a rescue dog" he said. "Rescue dog rescued me." I smiled my understanding as he waved at us and rode away.

Rescue dog Rescued me. I agree. Thank you Phoenix. Thank you all.

~Grateful Mommy Jenny

Jenny's words on Facebook on July 19[th:]

Phoenix and Chester update!

Hi everyone!! Thank you for all your sweet messages and checking in on us!! We're all doing GREAT and appreciating all our special moments together. It was bath day today so BOTH boys smell like HEAVEN which is great news for ME since I love to snuggle and kiss on them both!

Chester has his normal energy back (normal for the little old dude that he is!) and I'm thrilled. We'll see the vet next week for more x-rays and when his lungs are clear we can discontinue the plethora of meds he is on right now. Yay! Healing Healing!

And speaking of Healing! Our little PHOENIX is healing up amazingly well also! We still have a few more weeks before we see the vet but he is using that paw to run, play, and hug so I have a REALLY good feeling that he will keep the leg. I really can't imagine otherwise at this point.

You prayer warriors have worked MIRACLES in the lives of both of these boys and I am so grateful for you!!! I hope everyone has a great weekend. We love you!

~Jenny, Phoenix, and Chester!!

Jenny's words on Facebook on July 27th:

Phoenix and Chester Update!

Hello everyone! Thank you so much for all your prayers and for keeping in touch with us! Phoenix, Chester, and I are so grateful for your love, tips, ideas, and stories!!!!

Chester went to the vet yesterday. The pneumonia is

only 1/2 way cleared out of his lungs. She said it could take 6-8 weeks to clear! Yikes! It's only been 3. So for now we keep him on the antibiotics and humidifier and we'll do another lung x-ray in 2 weeks. Fingers and paws crossed that it will be a clear one by then! Otherwise he seems GREAT. Chester has got energy and he's happy. He seems to have a whole new lease on life now that he has a baby brother.

Phoenix is doing great too! His leg is fantastic!! He has sensation in it and he can use it which means... he can keep it!!! HOOORAY!!!!

Yesterday he PROVED how well that leg works to me! After a super long walk he busted out of his collar and made a run for it when we got back to the house! He was clearly NOT DONE with that walk! I chased him down the block where he ran straight to the house of his other two favorite dogs and pawed at their door. I was able to snatch him up there and take him home with a good talk about how he can't run away. There are too many people that love him now!! He just loves to be social and couldn't understand why we weren't going to visit his friends, but it certainly scared ME!!! We're still establishing boundaries, trust, all of that. He's so happy here, but he is so social too. I'm trying to strike that balance with him between fun and training. We might have to do a dog park run before his surgery Monday so he can RUN RUN RUN!! He really needs that now!

He's getting fixed on Monday but no leg removed!! Whoohooo!!! He's sitting with me here now... still apologizing for scaring me yesterday. What a precious little dude.

OK, we're off on another walk! Much love to each of you and your fur babies too. We'd love to hear stories about your pups also. Any great adventures planned this weekend??

Many blessings and much love

~Jenny, Phoenix, and Chester!!

Jenny's words on Facebook on July 28th:

In between moments of tearing up all the toys I get precious moments to snuggle this sweet boy. Phoenix is getting fixed tomorrow! Neutered that is. Little he knows.... yet! I'm snuggling him up like crazy today though and giving him lots of healing love in advance for tomorrow morning's surgery!!! LOVE this doggie so MUCH!!!

Jenny's words on Facebook on July 29th:

All strapped into the car and ready for the vet! I took Phoenix into Dr. Mark today at 7:30am and they said he should be done by Noon! Whoohoo!! Phoenix is SUPER excited to see Ms. Toby today and then of course come home to Mommy and Chester. He was such a good boy on the way in. He has no fear. Such a brave guy! I'm missing fighting over the keyboard with him this morning!! Hurry home Phoenix!!! We love you SO MUCH!!!

~Mommy Jenny and Brother Chester

Jenny's words on Facebook on July 29th:

Phoenix and Dr. Mark did GREAT today!! He was yelping and crying until mama rounded the corner and then all was right in his world... besides the swirly walls and dancing elephants. "Stop reminding me of elephants, Ms Toby!" He's home and sleeping soundly with his brother now. Two peas in a pod! Thank you for all the prayers. Phoenix is DONE with surgeries for now!!! He's keeping that paw which is doing just fine. What an amazing guy.

Jenny's words on Facebook on July 30th:

Phoenix is recovering well from surgery. He is REALLY red and swollen, which I guess happens with some dogs. We went back to see the Doc this morning and Phoenix got a shot of an anti inflammatory med and a pain killer to last 24hrs. He's not acting too bothered, but it looks CRAZY painful!! I think he's more bothered with the cone. He also hasn't let me out of his sight except when I had to leave for a few hours of work today. I think yesterday scared him to be back at the vet and away from me. I'm reminding him constantly today that he won't lose me. We're together forever now! He's been holding on tighter than ever in those hugs. We have indeed BONDED!!!

Chester is doing great. Slow and steady healing for that boy. Still on the mend and still on the meds which is challenging to this holistic Mommy's sensibilities AND pocketbook but I know he needs them and I know they are doing the trick. So I bless them and pop 'em in his mouth with gratitude that I still have him with me.

That's the thing... Money and energy come and go... But these moments that you can remember and treasure and be fully present to how much love there is available to us... that's the good stuff! The doggies, for me, are the key to remembering how much love is available to each of us and the moments with them are like grace. I couldn't be a luckier or more blessed dog mom.

Thank you each for loving us and sharing your lives and doggie stories with us too! We love to hearing about you and your fur kids as well.

Much love to you each from Jenny, Phoenix, and Chester

Jenny's words on Facebook on Aug 17th:

Phoenix just had me fall over laughing so hard that I was crying!! He has these two little tennis balls that we play with. I squeak one and throw it and then he brings it back while I throw the other and then he goes after it. Two days ago the orange ball went missing. Tonight we were playing with the green one alone until it bounced against the wall and shot under the bed. Phoenix chased it under the bed and in perfect comic timing emerged immediately with not the green ball but the orange ball. Mystery solved! THAT'S where they hide or where Phoenix hides them more likely! HAHAHAHA. What a funny doggie!!!

Jenny's words on Facebook on Oct 16th:

The boys are doing great! Chester is lost and confused a lot these days but he just still seems so happy every time he finds me or BBP or food. I trust he will continue to let me know the best ways to support him in his old age.

BBP is fantastic. He plays HARD and loves hard daily! He jumps off the back of the couch and lands square on that front leg without a flinch. I'm trying to convince him not to do that but I think he likes to fly and it doesn't seem to hurt him. I've been working on some training with him and he is SO GOOD at walking right by my side on our walks now even when he's super excited and wants to be crazy. He's such a good listener and such a love. He sleeps on my chest or pressed against my back or pressed against Chester. The back of the couch is his favorite new spot. Up high enough to look out the window and never have to miss a thing! The other day I came home and Chester had pooped and then spun in circles walking in it until he had made a poop labyrinth across my hard wood floors. BBP ran back and forth on the back of the couch, not jumping down, as if to say, "Help me Mom! I can't go down there!" I carried both dogs to the back yard where they got to hang out while I worked my way from the outside in to the poop labyrinth with my cleaning supplies. Oh the joys of being a dog mom!

Haha! I wouldn't trade it for anything!! I love these two so much. Thank you all for loving us too! I hope you are all having a great week!

Lots of Love from Jenny, BBP, and Chester!!!

Jenny's words on Facebook on Dec 1st:

Jenny, BBP, and Chester Update

Happy Holidays everyone! Thank you so much for your amazing messages, love, notes, and prayers!!!

Chester is doing great! I swear if you ask this community to pray, healing happens.... and fast! I know he is old and we really are appreciating every moment.... but earlier this week I really thought "this is it." He was in pain and crying and yelping to the touch. Two days of that and I thought... we just have to get through the weekend to get to Dr. Mark. Phoenix snuggled him and I massaged his little back and legs and YOU all prayed and yesterday and today he is acting perfectly fine and taking regular walks between his bowl and Phoenix's bowl to make sure he isn't missing any morsels of life giving turkey that might fall in those dishes! I think he and Phoenix both know a thing or two about being cats and having 9-900 lives in them!

Phoenix is also amazing and such a love. I had to have a tooth drilled today and he came with me to the dentist. He goes straight into the arms of the girls at the front desk and loves on everyone there until I'm done. He sat on the desk and greeted people and I could hear so much joy and laughter coming from the other room which was healing, calming, and heartwarming for me too. He brings joy and comfort everywhere he goes. Then when I came out of the room he ran straight into my arms and held on tight as if to say, "That was fun, Mom, but let's go now!" Haha. What an angel pie love.

Every day I tell him that I didn't think I could love him any more but here it is... another day... and I do.

We love each of you and are so honored that you love us too. Thank you for your love and prayers. Wishing the best of life to all of you and yours this holiday season.

~Jenny, BBP, and Chester

Chapter 15
THROUGH THE EYES OF DOG

"If I were a dog, I'd want you for my mommy!"

~Caron Finner-Garcia

Jenny:

I'm fairly intuitive and I pick up on lot of telepathic communications, most especially from my own animals.

Phoenix doesn't talk about his past life or anything he's gone through. He only speaks as far back as Toby, Dr. Hart and Dr. Mark and the vet techs, then lots about me and Chester. Mostly he talks about life now. He speaks of walks and car rides and treats and toys and love, the occasional twig in his fur, or the absolute fact that baths are abhorrent but tolerable only because he trusts me and knows treats come after along with lots of cuddles. He tells me about what and who he loves and what he thinks now, not about what used to be.

But one day on a walk as we were communing with nature and each other, he told me that he almost died.

"I know" I said in my head to him, surprised to hear him communicate anything about his life before he became the happy and famous little star, Baby Boy Phoenix, the dog who rose from the ashes.

"I'm so glad you didn't die, sweet angel boy, but what made you decide to stay?"

"You" he said. "The great spirit of DOG promised me you."

Chapter 16
THE GIFT IS IN THE PRESENT

"His former life has been forgotten by BBP, thank goodness! I do believe it was divine intervention for him to get to you via Toby. Love this dog! What a story his life has been!"

~Joyce Grossman

Phoenix:

I don't like to talk about my life before my rescue. Everyone saw the results of my previous life and that was hard enough on everyone. I love people and I don't want to stress them out with stories that mean nothing to me anymore. There is so much good to talk about now... and love. I find I don't have any room for sadness when there is so much to be grateful for. My mommy and Ms. Toby tell me that I don't act mad or sad or injured anymore because dogs live in the present.

I guess they are right. My new life of love is like a gift, a really great present, and I wouldn't want to live anywhere else but here!

Love always and all~ways.... Lucky me.

~BBP

ABOUT THE AUTHOR

Jenny Karns is a writer, healer, storyteller, coach, teacher, speaker, mentor, avid dreamer, and animal lover. She is the founder of Body Temple Healing, a thriving Los Angeles based healing practice, and the creator of the smash hit telesummit, Remembering Our Magic, which has helped thousands of women globally to heal what holds them back, harness their unique gifts, and take those gifts global.

Jenny is also the founder of Dreality Press, a publishing house that inspires dreams to become reality through books and products that uplift and inspire. She is the author of the book, *Baby Boy Phoenix; a Tale of Rescue, Love, and Second Chances*, and the forthcoming book, *Alchemy and the Ache; Transforming Life's Pain Into Power.*

Jenny is passionate about helping the animals and is giving 10% of the proceeds of this book to local rescues, including Leave No Paws Behind, to whom she owes a huge debt of gratitude for gifting her with Baby Boy Phoenix.

For more on information on Jenny Karns please visit: www.JennyKarns.com

To continue following Baby Boy Phoenix's journey, go to: www.BabyBoyPhoenix.com

Or follow Phoenix on facebook at: www.facebook.com/BabyBoyPhoenix

To donate directly to Leave no Paws Behind and follow their other amazing rescue stories please visit: www.leavenopawsbehind.org

31738402R00058

Made in the USA
Lexington, KY
23 April 2014